This journal belongs to

....

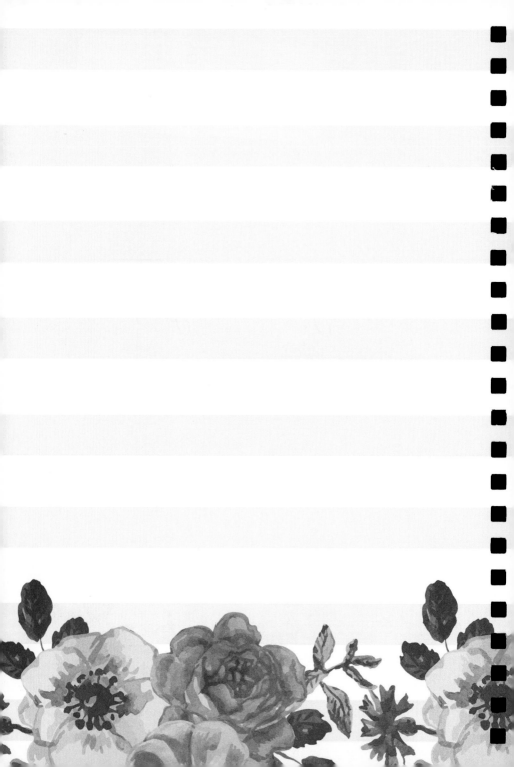

The
30-Day
Prayer
Challenge
JOURNAL
for Women

NICOLE O'DELL

BARBOUR BOOKS
An Imprint of Barbour Publishing, Inc.

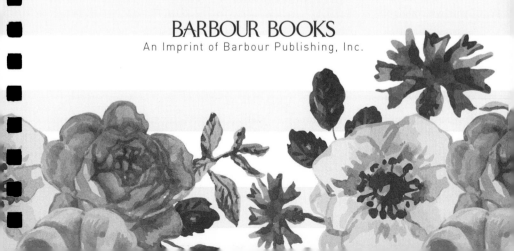

INTRODUCTION

Welcome to *The 30-Day Prayer Challenge for Women!*

After a daily reading that will help you see things the way God does, there are some questions to help you learn from your own thoughts and experiences about that topic. Do your best to be honest as you explore your answers, because that's the only way to really grow. Your responses to those questions will help you apply the truth to your life. Then, three prayer focuses—morning, afternoon, and evening—will keep you thinking and praying about that topic all day so it will take root in your heart.

The thirty days of focus will show you how important and beneficial it is to be in the Word of God daily and how much of an impact regular prayer times will have on your life. Pay attention to how your attitudes and expectations are changed as you spend time with Jesus and how you begin to look forward to that time each day. Plan now to take those practices forward beyond these thirty days and make them a part of the rest of your life.

Day 1

NO SURPRISES

*Those who think they know something do
not yet know as they ought to know.*
1 Corinthians 8:2 NIV

Some things seem so clear. In those cases, it's easy for us to see the right choice because it's so obviously best for us and others. Of course it's the right move to take the new job. Of course it's a good thing to buy that new house. Of course it's a positive thing to say yes to your pastor's ministry request. After all, a good thing must be the right thing, right? If you're like me, you often find yourself operating on that kind of logic and then feeling shocked when things get derailed or God says no.

About a year ago, I was looking for a job and made it to the very end of the interviewing process for one that seemed so perfect for me. The work was right in my wheelhouse, and the business was next door to my actual house! How could that not be God's plan for me? Well, it came down to me and one other person. Guess who got the job? Someone who'd have to drive thirty minutes to get there. Was God sleeping on the job? He must have been to let that one slip through.

Honestly, I was devastated. Didn't He care that I needed to make more money and that me being that close to home would be better for my kids? He was silent. But it wasn't very long before another opportunity presented itself. It was a better job, with better pay, and an even better location—my home office. I got that job and was reminded that even when I think I know best, God knows more. If I'd gotten the first one, I'd have stopped looking and would have missed out on His perfect will and provision.

WHAT'S UP?

- What ideal are you holding on to that you need to put in God's hands?

....

....

....

....

- How can you change your approach to decisions to allow more room for God's perfect will?

....

....

....

....

....

- List some big things that you'll be planning in the short and long term, and write a sentence or two to help you consider God's will.

....

....

....

....

PRAYER PROMPTS

Morning: Pray that God will give you peace when you face tough choices.

Something like this. . .

> *Dear God, thank You for being there with me when*
> *I have to make difficult decisions. Please help me seek*
> *Your guidance even when the way seems clear to me.*
> *I want to follow You in all things. Amen.*

Afternoon: Ask God to show you His plan.

Something like this. . .

> Father, I want to walk in Your will, but it's difficult when I don't know what it is. Would You help me to learn to follow Your leading with eagerness and grace, even when I don't get it? And please show me when You've been working on my behalf so I can understand. Amen.

....

....

....

....

....

....

....

....

....

....

....

....

....

....

Evening: Ask Him to settle your spirit when surprises come.

Something like this. . .

> Lord, it's hard to let go of what I want and to accept
> when things don't work out according to what seems
> best to me. Please calm my spirit when I face those
> surprises so I can see where You're at work. Amen.

Day 2

FANNING THE FLAMES

Where there is no fuel a fire goes out; where there is no gossip arguments come to an end.
PROVERBS 26:20 CEV

That verse paints such a vivid image. I can see the flames of a fire reaching for something to burn. When it runs out of fuel or flammable objects, the fire dies because there's nothing to feed it. The same is true for gossip. It starts as a small fire, looking for fuel—ears that will listen and lips that will share. The fire of gossip craves attention, and it will die without it. If no one listens to it, there's no one to spread it, so it naturally fades away.

I have special friends who have seen me through some of the darkest moments of my life. They've been there with me through everything, and I know I can trust them with anything. We see things the same way, and we love to share stories and compare experiences. We also pray for each other and trade prayer requests all the time. That is all part of the wonderful, godly gift of friendship. The problem is, we are so close and trust each other so much, that sometimes that intimacy can stoke the fires of gossip until it's a raging bonfire.

Commit to yourself that you won't participate in being the gossip sharer, listener, or spreader. Let the juicy tidbits of someone else's life and experiences die in your mouth rather than sharing destructive information for selfish gain. Take that commitment to your friends and family, and ask them to help you make the change by supporting you when you resist the urge to gossip. When you do that, they will see your effort and perhaps become convicted to make a similar commitment for themselves. Start an epidemic!

WHAT'S UP?

- How does God feel about gossip? Why?

....

....

....

....

- How does gossip destroy relationships?

....

....

....

....

....

- When have you gossiped and caused someone pain? Do you need to seek reconciliation from that person?

....

....

....

....

....

PRAYER PROMPTS

Morning: Pray that God will help you hold your tongue when you're tempted to gossip.

Something like this. . .

> *Dear God, please seal my lips when I have something to say about someone else. Help me not to take pleasure in sharing things that are none of my business. Amen.*

....

....

....

....

....

....

....

....

....

....

....

....

Afternoon: Ask God to replace your desire to gossip with good
works.

Something like this. . .

> *Dear God, I recognize that I've spent a lot of time talking*
> *about other people. Please help me resist that but also*
> *to use the energy I've spent on gossip for Your good.*
> *Show me ways I can be a light to the people*
> *I would have once talked about. Amen.*

Evening: Ask Him to show you the gossip fodder in your life.

Something like this. . .

> *Father, it's always easy to see the flaws in others.*
> *Please blind me to the faults in those around me*
> *and, instead, help me see the areas where*
> *I need growth in my own life. Amen.*

....

....

....

....

....

....

....

....

....

....

....

....

....

....

....

....

....

EXPECTATIONS

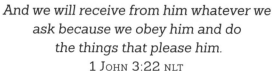

And we will receive from him whatever we
ask because we obey him and do
the things that please him.
1 John 3:22 NLT

Babies are born with an innate expectation that they will be taken care of. They learn that crying gets them fed, cleaned, or rocked. Toddlers expect their wants and needs to be met immediately, and they will throw a tantrum if they don't get their way. They don't negotiate; they have no patience; and they don't take no for an answer. As we get older, we learn that things don't always go our way. But that's not always easy!

God tells us that we can have whatever we want, we just need to ask and He'll deliver. Right? Not exactly. That verse above and others like it that talk about God's provision and generosity are often misquoted. The perception is that if we ask, we get. But check out the end of that verse: "because we obey him and do the things that please him." That doesn't mean that He'll always say yes to reward us. It means that because we are in His will, we will want what He wants for us.

It is unnatural for a child to look at a parent and ask permission to cross a busy street without looking—that request is a contradiction with the will of the parent for the child. It is natural, however, for that child to ask for help with homework or for a second helping of a healthy dinner. When we are seeking God's will for our lives, it's natural to ask Him to show us what we need and to make our desires line up with His. There's no better feeling, as a woman of God, to know that we are chasing Him with our whole heart and expecting great things according to His will.

WHAT'S UP?

- What is on your list of wants right now? Do they line up with God's will or your own?

....

....

....

....

....

- How do you handle it when God says no or not yet?

....

....

....

....

- What do you need to let go of so you can get closer to God's will for you?

....

....

....

....

....

PRAYER PROMPTS

Morning: Pray that God will give you gratitude.

Something like this. . .

> *Dear God, I'm sorry that I've grumbled when things haven't gone my way. Please remind me of all the ways You've blessed me, and help me practice gratitude all day today. Amen.*

....

....

....

....

....

....

....

....

....

....

....

....

....

Afternoon : Ask God to help you line your desires with His will.

Something like this. . .

> *Dear Lord, I want what You want for me because I know
> it's the very best plan and the only way to find true peace.
> Please help me trust You even when You say no. Amen.*

Evening: Ask Him to show you what you need to let go of.

Something like this. . .

> *Father, I've tried to do a lot of things my own way,*
> *and I've chased what I thought would fulfill me. Please help*
> *me now to lay down my own will, let go of the treasures*
> *of this world, and follow Your heart in all things. Amen.*

GOD'S ECONOMY

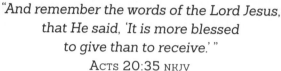

*"And remember the words of the Lord Jesus,
that He said, 'It is more blessed
to give than to receive.'"*
ACTS 20:35 NKJV

There's a woman at my church whose generosity has spoken to me over the years. I've watched her do things for people and give money and possessions away so effortlessly, expecting nothing in return. My guess is that she gives more than anyone really knows. Generosity just flows from her. I talked to her about it once. I asked how she could be so free with her money, her possessions, and even her time. She said, "Sweetie, it's all God's economy. I'm just a funnel so He can get it where He wants it."

Years later I found out that she really doesn't have much herself. She makes little money and has very few possessions. She finds her joy in giving. It's easy to give of our resources when they are spilling over, isn't it? But the true expression of faith-filled generosity is when we give with abandon and in obedience whether we have a surplus or not.

In 2 Corinthians 8:2 (TLB), Paul refers to the Macedonian church: "Though they have been going through much trouble and hard times, they have mixed their wonderful joy with their deep poverty, and the result has been an overflow of giving to others." That explains why that friend of mine has so much joy. It's a byproduct of generosity.

This can't be your end goal, but do you realize that the more generous you are, the more you will be given because you can be trusted with it? You can show your faith by giving more and watching what God does.

WHAT'S UP?

- How do you feel about your own spirit of generosity?

....

....

....

....

- What financial (or other) burdens keep you from being generous?

....

....

....

....

- What are two or three steps you can take to begin to position yourself as a funnel for God's economy?

....

....

....

....

....

PRAYER PROMPTS

Morning: Pray for financial direction.

Something like this. . .

> *Dear God, will You show me today where I'm missing the mark as a steward of Your economy? Show me what I need to change in my financial habits and my lifestyle so I can be more generous. Amen.*

....

....

....

....

....

....

....

....

....

....

....

....

....

....

Afternoon : Ask God to give you the faith to be generous.

Something like this. . .

> *Dear God, You've never failed me. I've always had what I need. Please help me have the faith to let go of the control of my money and things. Help me to give with abandon when You call me to. Amen.*

Evening: Pray for opportunity.

Something like this. . .

> *Father, thank You for leading me to greater generosity.
> I'm ready! Please show me opportunities where You would
> have me funnel some of Your goodness to others. Amen.*

Day 5

JOIN GOD

But Jesus told him, "Anyone who puts a hand
to the plow and then looks back is not
fit for the Kingdom of God."
LUKE 9:62 NLT

God is today. He is now. He is here, present, with us. His heart is not in the past and, although He knows the future, He's not there waiting for us to arrive. He's here.

It's not wrong to plan ahead and prepare for the future. But worrying about tomorrow is pointless. Tomorrow will have joy and pain, success and failure, no matter how much you worry. And worry reveals a lack of faith. If you don't believe that God has tomorrow in the palm of His hand and has your very best interests at heart, then you will worry. But if you believe in who He is and what He wants for you, then you will be at peace about the future, confident that it will be perfect because you've surrendered to His will.

Even worse than fearing the future is to regret the past which only cripples us for tomorrow. Did you know that our Father chooses to forget our pasts once we've turned them over to Him? He truly forgives and forgets, and though our sins were like scarlet, He makes them white as snow. So, if He chooses not to stay mired in the mistakes we made, why do we insist on doing it? It's because our enemy wants us to feel discouraged and unworthy so we don't boldly step into the calling God has for us in the present. The last thing your enemy wants is for you to believe in your identity in Christ and share that good news with others. So, if he can keep you mired in guilt, you won't move forward in the kingdom. Shut him down, and join God in the work He's doing today.

WHAT'S UP?

- What mistakes have you made that keep you from truly trusting in God's grace? Write them down.

....

....

....

....

....

- How has your guilt and shame kept you from participating in God's work?

....

....

....

....

....

- Where is God working around you right now? How can you join Him?

....

....

....

....

PRAYER PROMPTS

Morning: Pray that God will show you how guilt is working in your life.

Something like this. . .

Dear God, there are mistakes in my past, and sometimes they keep me from truly trusting You. Please show me how my clinging to the past and not trusting in Your grace keeps me from what You have for me. Amen.

....

....

....

....

....

....

....

....

....

....

....

....

....

Afternoon: Ask God to heal you from regret.

Something like this. . .

> *Dear God, now that I see where guilt has a hold on me, please heal me from it. Help me to, once and for all, cast my regret aside and keep me from grabbing it back so I can move forward with You, unhindered by the past. Amen.*

....

....

....

....

....

....

....

....

....

....

....

....

....

....

....

....

....

....

Evening: Ask God to teach you from your past.

Something like this. . .

> *Father, even though You don't want me to struggle with guilt, I know You want me to learn. Please show me the lessons You want me to learn from the experiences I've had so I can apply them to the future and help others who might face something similar. Amen.*

....
....
....
....
....
....
....
....
....
....
....
....
....
....
....
....
....

Day 6

QUICK TO LISTEN

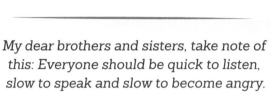

*My dear brothers and sisters, take note of
this: Everyone should be quick to listen,
slow to speak and slow to become angry.*
JAMES 1:19 NIV

Have you ever been embroiled in a deep conversation or debate and you know you're making good points, but you can tell the other person is just waiting for the noise to stop so she can talk? It's frustrating because the conversation is one-sided and basically pointless. Or how about when you're asking friends for help or sharing some pain, but all they want to do is top your story with one of their own? You don't feel heard or supported in those moments at all, do you?

God calls us to be quick to listen, which means our first response is to try to hear and understand. In fact, the verse above addresses the listening part of communication before the speaking and emotional parts. Listening, by its nature, is an open posture. It is taking in not putting out.

Be patient when you talk with people. Don't be so intent on making your point or being right that you miss an opportunity to share and learn. Hear the words people say so you can understand their heart and meet their needs.

WHAT'S UP?

- What does it mean to be quick to listen? How would that look in your interactions?

....

....

....

....

- What is a time when you've rushed to speak and it broke down communication? How could that have looked different?

....

....

....

....

- How can you train yourself to listen first and fully rather than jump to speech or judgment?

....

....

....

....

PRAYER PROMPTS

Morning: Pray that God will slow your tongue.

Something like this. . .

> *Dear God, my mouth gets ahead of my brain and my heart so often. Please slow me down and help me control my speech to make me in tune with the communication of the Holy Spirit. Amen.*

....

....

....

....

....

....

....

....

....

....

....

....

....

....

Afternoon: Ask Him to open your ears.

Something like this...

> *Dear God, I want to be quick to listen. I want people to feel heard by me. Please help me slow down and take time. Open my ears and help me hear first from You and then from others. Amen.*

Evening; Pray for wisdom in your response.

Something like this. . .

> *Father, now that I'm listening more and seeking to understand, help my response to be in line with You. Please show me how to respond in godly, righteous ways to the needs of others.*
> *Let me be an extension of Your hand. Amen.*

....

....

....

....

....

....

....

....

....

....

....

....

....

....

Day 7

TIME MANAGEMENT

Look carefully then how you walk, not as unwise but as wise, making the best use of the time, because the days are evil.
Ephesians 5:15–16 esv

Women are, by nature, great multitaskers. We keep a lot of things going at once, and most of the time we do it well. Sometimes though, we overestimate our abilities and underestimate our limitations and pack our lives with too much. We say yes to every request made of us and then find ourselves scrambling to do anything with excellence and resenting others along the way. I know that's very true for me. I get my life and my schedule so packed to the brim that I find myself trying to rush through important things just to keep a promise or make a deadline or not disappoint someone. And then I'm annoyed with the people who "forced" me to take on so much.

The Lord wants us to use our time wisely for His purposes. We can't do that when we're overcommitted. He also wants us to do our very best with everything we take on. We can't do that when we're rushing through life. He wants us freed up enough that when a real need arises, there's enough margin in our lives that we can meet it. It takes intentional planning and focus to protect your time and make yourself available.

Jesus never missed a chance to do what was right, but He also knew He had to protect His spiritual well-being and went to quiet places to pray. He was wise enough to feed His soul with rest so He would be ready to do His Father's work. In the same way, we can feed our souls with prayer, worship, and meditation on scripture. Then we will be prepared and open for whatever comes up.

WHAT'S UP?

- Name a few things that you're committed to that stress you out, are out of your wheelhouse, or don't line up with God's plan for you.

....

....

....

....

- How did you find yourself committed to those things? What was the motivation?

....

....

....

....

- How can you take back your schedule and manage your time better? How can you avoid that trap in the future?

....

....

....

....

PRAYER PROMPTS

Morning: Pray that God will help you manage your time better.
Something like this. . .

> *Dear God, I have good intentions, and it feels good to say*
> *yes to everything, but I know I need more margin*
> *and rest. Please help me to see what I need to*
> *change about my life right now. Amen.*

Afternoon : Ask God to give you time management tools.

Something like this. . .

> *Dear God, the easiest way to have a healthy schedule is to not let it get out of hand in the first place. Please help me make wise choices about what I agree to, and give me the courage to say no when I need to. Help me to prioritize the important things. Amen.*

Evening: Ask Him to heal your body and mind from the stress.

Something like this...

> *Father, now that I'm making time for myself, I see the effect*
> *the stress has had on me. Please help my mind to settle*
> *and my body to relax from all the pressure.*
> *Help me find lasting peace. Amen.*

....

....

....

....

....

....

....

....

....

....

....

....

....

....

....

....

EYE OF THE BEHOLDER

*Your beauty should not come from outward adornment,
such as elaborate hairstyles and the wearing of gold jewelry
or fine clothes. Rather, it should be that of your inner
self, the unfading beauty of a gentle and quiet
spirit, which is of great worth in God's sight.*
1 PETER 3:3–4 NIV

Who are we trying to impress with all this striving to have the perfect body, perfect wardrobe, perfect face? Who is the judge of our beauty, and how did we fall into the trap of that striving anyway? We work so hard to gain the approval of others, but they don't even think twice about us as they are trapped in their own world of striving too.

If I could add up all the time and mental anguish I've spent trying to achieve some kind of worldly ideal, I'd probably be sick. Take exercise for example. There was a time in my life when I spent hours at the gym for the sole purpose of looking better. But there came a point in my life when my focus shifted. Exercise became a joy because it invigorated me. It had become about performance and fun and health not appearance.

You, lovely friend, were made in the image of God. Beautiful in His sight. Recognized for the beauty that lasts—the unfading beauty that can only be found in a gentle spirit. Let go of the world's ideals for your physical appearance and your pursuit of a to-the-minute trendy wardrobe. Be thankful, instead, for the beautiful qualities that God planted within you. The ones that are of great worth in His sight.

WHAT'S UP?

- What are some unhealthy ways you've struggled with the pursuit of physical beauty?

....

....

....

....

- List three qualities that God has planted within you that are far more beautiful than outward appearance.

....

....

....

....

- How can you use those qualities to make a difference in the lives of others?

....

....

....

....

PRAYER PROMPTS

Morning: Pray that God will show you how He sees you.

Something like this. . .

> *Dear Jesus, please help me to see myself through Your eyes. Show me where You place the most value so I can focus there too. Amen.*

....

....

....

....

....

....

....

....

....

....

....

....

Afternoon : Ask God to forgive you.

Something like this. . .

> *Dear God, please forgive me for being so self-absorbed and focused on something that doesn't matter. I don't want to waste another minute in an unhealthy pursuit of a physical ideal just to hope for the approval of others. I love what You see in me, and that's the only approval I need. Amen.*

Evening: Ask Him to help you find balance.

Something like this. . .

> *Father, I know things like looking nice and exercising aren't*
> *inherently wrong. Please help me find a healthy balance so*
> *I can be a good steward of my body and my resources*
> *and a testimony to others about true beauty. Amen.*

Day 9

QUIET TIME

In the morning, LORD, you hear my
voice; in the morning I lay my requests
before you and wait expectantly.
PSALM 5:3 NIV

"You must have a quiet time with God every morning for at least thirty minutes. And for the spiritually mature, it would last an hour; but don't worry, you'll get there." Have you ever felt like that's the message you're hearing about having alone time with God? That kind of expected structure always fell short of inspiring me, that's for sure.

Yes, I think the morning is the best time to find those moments to pray, meditate, and study. It's often when the house is the quietest and the pressures of the day haven't crowded all the time yet, and it sets the tone for facing the mayhem. And, yes, I think we should dedicate a good chunk of the day to having that time with God. But I don't think He intends for us to set an alarm or stare at our watches. How would we feel if our kids or friends did that when they spent time with us? And is length of quiet time the measure of spiritual maturity? Not at all. The Pharisees had plenty of time to study and pray, yet they were the epitome of spiritual immaturity.

It comes down to this: How can you know Him unless you spend time with Him? How can He teach you unless you sit at His feet? How can He heal you of your pain unless you hand it over to Him? And how can you grow unless you spend time thanking Him and praising Him? Those things inspire me. That's what makes me open my Bible, sing out a praise song, or fall to my knees in prayer.

WHAT'S UP?

- How would you describe your intimacy with God?

....

....

....

....

- Do you believe that it's important to have a quiet time with God? What inspires you to do that?

....

....

....

....

....

- How can you better structure your day so you can have more alone time with God?

....

....

....

....

....

PRAYER PROMPTS

Morning: Have an extended time with God.

Something like this. . .

> *Dear God, I want to sit here at Your feet and rest. I want to hear You speak to me this morning so I can take that peace with me throughout my day. Help me hear You. Amen.*

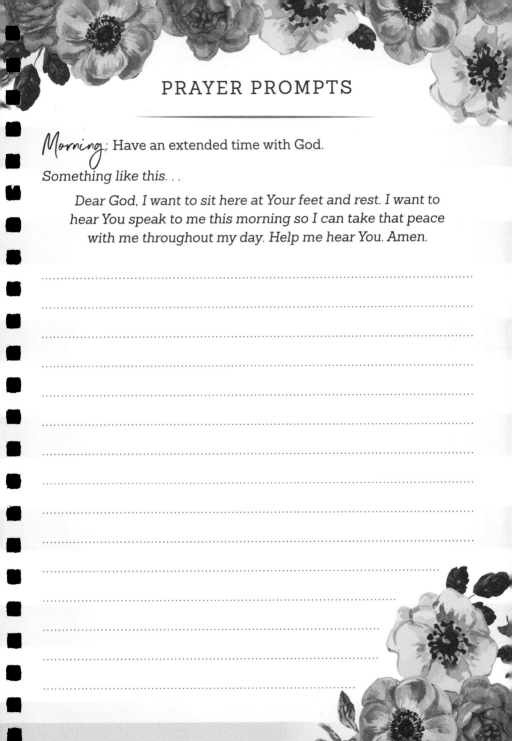

Afternoon : Ask God for a refreshing touch.

Something like this. . .

> *Jesus, as my day goes on, You feel further and further away. Please help me to stay near to You even in the midst of the chaos around me. Amen.*

Evening: Ask Him to speak to your heart in your rest.

Something like this. . .

> *Father, I love these days when I draw close to You.*
> *Please speak to my soul as I sleep, and wake*
> *me with eagerness to seek You and spend*
> *time with You in the morning. Amen.*

Day 10

SHOESTRING BUDGET

Wisdom is better when it's paired with money,
especially if you get both while you're still living.
Double protection: wisdom and wealth!
ECCLESIASTES 7:11–12 MSG

My pastor, who has since gone on to his heavenly reward, used to say, "If you show me the state of the inside of your car, I can tell you the state of your checkbook." What he was saying was that how we take care of, or steward, the things we are entrusted with is a revelation of how we steward all of God's resources. The first time I heard him say that, I realized he was right. My life at that time was a big rush—rush to the next event, rush to work out, rush to get dinner done, rush to get to sleep. In the midst of all the mayhem, I let things like the state of my car; the floor of my closet; the inside of my purse; and, yes, the condition of my checking account take a backseat to all the stuff I "had" to do.

In reality, it all comes down to the need for godly stewardship of our lives. Is your checkbook in order? How about the mountain of bills that gather on your desk? Is there a comfortable balance of savings, expenses, entertainment, and generosity? Or do you need to take steps to get your finances under control? If you are not operating with a budget, it may be time to start.

The most important thing in setting a budget is to be honest about your income and output. Recognize where you're overspending, and prioritize first things first. God asks for a portion of the firstfruits of our labor. Pray about what He'd have you do with your giving. Next, pay off interest-accruing debt, because you're a slave to that until it's gone. Last, build up a healthy savings account. It's time to fully surrender your finances to the Lord. It's okay for you to have things and money, but it's not okay when they have a hold on you because of debt or greed.

WHAT'S UP?

- Describe your financial situation.

....

....

....

....

- What are some financial mistakes you've made? What would you do differently next time?

....

....

....

....

....

- What are some very specific changes you can make to your money-management style that will have long-term effects on your finances?

....

....

....

....

PRAYER PROMPTS

Morning: Pray that God will help you make good financial decisions today.

Something like this. . .

> *Dear God, sometimes it seems like everyone wants money, and it's hard to balance my own needs and wants with everything else. Please help me make good choices today and be a good steward of all You've given me. Amen.*

....
....
....
....
....
....
....
....
....
....
....
....
....
....

Afternoon: Ask God to help you budget.

Something like this. . .

> *Dear God, it's clear I need some help in the area of my finances. Please help me set some guidelines for spending and to be diligent about my bills and other expenses. Help me to set a budget and stick to it. Amen.*

....

....

....

....

....

....

....

....

....

....

....

....

....

....

Evening: Ask Him to give you His perspective.

Something like this. . .

> *Father, I know You have a big-picture plan for my financial choices. Help me to make good choices now so there's room for me to join You in Your work. Amen.*

Day 11

MENTORSHIP

*Older women likewise are to be reverent in their behavior,
not malicious gossips nor enslaved to much wine,
teaching what is good.*
TITUS 2:3 NASB

There is always someone who has gone before you and someone coming behind you. It's a great system that God has set up so we can learn and teach at the same time. There's a woman in my life, Pam, who is very clearly a God-ordained mentor to me. She has been a vital part of my life since I was fourteen, and she has remained my spiritual guide ever since. I am able to be honest with her about my struggles, and she challenges me to do the right thing and make godly choices. She is my example for godly living in all areas of life. And there are others who look up to me in similar ways, which inspires me to stay close to Jesus so I don't let them down.

It's natural for women to cling to each other—we don't have to work at that as hard as the guys do. But we still must be intentional about pursuing those kinds of relationships and nurturing them until they develop into something trust-filled and lasting. The right mentor for you will have walked some of the same journey you have, will understand your hang-ups and your hurts, will not judge you for your weaknesses, and will inspire you to reach for new heights. Her job is to watch over you, pray for you, and speak truth to you. And your job is to be completely honest about your struggles, take in her advice and leadership, pray about how to apply it to your life, and then do the work to make it happen.

It's not easy to let your guard down, but once you do, you'll be so fulfilled by this special relationship.

WHAT'S UP?

- Whom do you consider a mentor in your life? What does she do that you respect and want to emulate?

....

....

....

....

- Who looks up to you as a mentor in her life? Are there others who could use your help either formally or informally?

....

....

....

- What are some lifestyle issues that you can address to make your life a better example to those who look up to you?

....

....

....

....

PRAYER PROMPTS

Morning: Pray for a mentor to come into your life.

Something like this. . .

> Father, I want to grow closer to You and live a more godly
> life as a woman. Please bring someone into my life who
> can share this journey with me and who can
> help guide me along the way. Amen.

....

....

....

....

....

....

....

....

....

....

....

....

....

....

Afternoon : Ask God to show you women he'd like you to mentor.

Something like this. . .

> *Dear God, please show me the women or girls You'd like*
> *me to pour my heart into in a special way. Help me to*
> *see them and understand their needs. Teach me*
> *how to lead them to You in all things. Amen.*

Evening: Ask Him to reveal areas of your life you need to strengthen so you can be a strong mentor.

Something like this. . .

Jesus, I know I'm not all the way there and that I have a long way to go. Please show me areas of my life You'd have me work on so I can be the leader You want me to be. Amen.

....
....
....
....
....
....
....
....
....
....
....
....
....
....
....
....
....

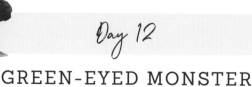

GREEN-EYED MONSTER

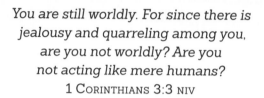

You are still worldly. For since there is
jealousy and quarreling among you,
are you not worldly? Are you
not acting like mere humans?
1 Corinthians 3:3 niv

Do you remember the story of David and Saul? Saul was so jealous of David that he made it his mission to kill him. He couldn't shake the hold that jealousy had on his heart. I had a boss once who was so jealous of the people who reported to her that she would sabotage their work in order to make herself look good. That made absolutely no sense because our work was a direct reflection on her as a manager, but she couldn't see it. She was so intent on looking like the only capable person around that she ended up destroying herself in the process. That kind of illogical behavior started as a little seed of self-doubt and grew into a life-controlling jealousy.

Jealousy will lead to tragedy every time. Maybe not murder but definitely lost or damaged relationships, damaged reputations, distrust, and misery. And it becomes a block between us and God. When we're so caught up in someone else that we are jealous of them, we can't see the truth or hear God's voice. Then jealousy has taken over.

The best way to get rid of jealousy in your life is to do good for the person you are jealous of. For example, if you are becoming jealous of someone's ministry, don't be like Saul; instead, encourage them in it. You could even take it one step further and offer to help. Once you do, you'll see those twinges of jealousy flee.

WHAT'S UP?

- When has jealousy become a problem for you?

....

....

....

....

- What seeds of jealousy are you dealing with right now?

....

....

....

....

- What are some ways to prevent jealousy from taking root?

....

....

....

....

PRAYER PROMPTS

Morning: Pray the Holy Spirit will convict you of jealousy.

Something like this. . .

> *Dear God, it's so easy to look around and want what others have. Please show me the jealousy I have in my heart. Amen.*

....

....

....

....

....

....

....

....

....

....

....

....

....

....

....

....

....

Afternoon: Ask God to heal relationships damaged by jealousy.

Something like this. . .

> Dear Jesus, please show me where I've let jealousy drive wedges or put limitations on relationships in my life. Help me restore them to a godly condition by confronting my own sin and seeking forgiveness where needed. Amen.

Evening: Pray for the strength to encourage rather than feel jealousy.

Something like this. . .

> *Father, You know where my jealousy has been strongest.*
> *Please give me the grace to be an encourager and a*
> *helper instead of grumbling and coveting. Amen.*

....

....

....

....

....

....

....

....

....

....

....

....

....

....

....

....

THE TREADMILL OF LIFE

And now, dear brothers and sisters, one final thing.
Fix your thoughts on what is true, and honorable, and right,
and pure, and lovely, and admirable. Think about things
that are excellent and worthy of praise.
PHILIPPIANS 4:8 NLT

"This is never going to get better." "I'm never going to make enough money." "My kid will never get into college." "I'll never lose weight." "No way I'm getting that promotion." Whatever the negative talk in your brain is shouting at you, it's probably on a loop. The same thoughts, with a few new ones sprinkled in as they develop, run through your mind all day long like the ticker tape in Times Square. It's an endless battle because one thought leads to another, and the fear builds to a crescendo.

I do triathlons, so I train in swimming, biking, and running. I love to swim and bike, but running is my least successful skill. Since I need more practice with it, I try to do it more often than the others. In the winter, here in Central Illinois, running outside isn't always an option, but, for me, running on the treadmill is the worst. There's no progress, no forward motion; it's a repetitive action, forced into one place, and there's no escape. When I run outside, I feel freer and enjoy the progress of the change in scenery and the forward motion. That summarizes our thought life, exactly. When we allow the negative to run constantly in our brains, it's like running on a treadmill—there's no forward progress, no relief, no escape.

Philippians 4:8 tells us to fix our minds on the positive things of God. Let go, take in the scenery, and move ahead. We're not to let our fears and struggles crowd out those truths. If we surrender our thought life to Him, God's mercy will cover our minds and turn our eyes to His grace.

WHAT'S UP?

- What do your negative thought patterns look like? Write some examples.

....

....

....

....

....

- Rewrite those thoughts into positive declarations.

....

....

....

....

....

- How can you discipline yourself to think on praiseworthy things rather than dwell on the negatives?

....

....

....

....

PRAYER PROMPTS

Morning: Pray that God will give you clarity today.

Something like this. . .

> *Dear God, I don't want to churn negativity today.*
> *Please help me see clearly when I start to worry or*
> *become negative. Stop me in my tracks so I can turn*
> *my thoughts to the positive things of You. Amen.*

Afternoon: Pray that God will protect your thoughts.

Something like this. . .

> *Dear God, please show me in each moment that You are*
> *on the throne of every one of my desires and fears.*
> *Let me trust in You so I can turn my fears to praise.*
> *Keep the doubts from taking hold. Amen.*

....

....

....

....

....

....

....

....

....

....

....

....

....

....

Evening: Ask God to turn your thoughts around completely.

Something like this. . .

> *Father, now that I see the need to get off the treadmill of my negative thinking, help me to turn my thoughts toward You, thinking only about praiseworthy things. Amen.*

Day 14

BIG MISTAKE

Brothers and sisters, if someone is caught in a sin, you who live by the Spirit should restore that person gently. But watch yourselves, or you also may be tempted. Carry each other's burdens, and in this way you will fulfill the law of Christ.
GALATIANS 6:1–2 NIV

I have been in situations when I've had to confront friends about some sin or misstep in their lives or share hurt that they had caused me or someone else. On the flip side of that, I've also been in situations when friends have had to confront me with the same kinds of things. Sometimes, true friendship means saying difficult things. Jesus showed by His example that we aren't to shy away from challenging others when it comes to righteousness. Confrontation is never fun, but we all need people in our lives who care about us enough to say what needs to be said, even if we don't want to hear it.

The notion that just because someone is a Christian she won't fail is one of the reasons so many people accuse Christians of being hypocrites. If we were capable of being perfect, we wouldn't have need of a Savior. So, with that fallacy aside, we can feel safe in confronting sin, if it's done in the name of Jesus and offered gently, with love.

In the end, no matter what the other person's response is, our goal should be to restore and encourage our loved ones to draw closer to God by eradicating sin. The goal isn't to blame or even get the person to admit their sin. It's simply to act as a voice of the Holy Spirit and then let Him do the rest. Be sure you have checked your motives and have a clean heart on the matter, have bathed the situation in prayer, approached the person with love, and left it in God's hands.

WHAT'S UP?

- When is it good to correct someone for sin?

....

....

....

....

....

- How can you go about offering the correction in a godly way?

....

....

....

....

....

- Is there someone you need to confront in your life right now? Write some points to provide structure and a goal for the conversation.

....

....

....

....

....

PRAYER PROMPTS

Morning: Pray that your heart is open to correction.

Something like this. . .

Dear God, I want to grow and learn how to live a more righteous life. Please soften my heart and make me open to correction. Give me discernment to know when the message I'm brought is from You. Amen.

....

....

....

....

....

....

....

....

....

....

....

....

....

....

....

Afternoon : Ask God to help you see where others need guidance on their journey.

Something like this. . .

> *Dear God, I care about my friends and loved ones and want to help them draw closer to You by making their lifestyles and choices more in line with Your will. Help me to see where I need to jump in and offer a word of correction. Amen.*

....

....

....

....

....

....

....

....

....

....

....

....

....

....

Evening: Pray that your heart will be right.

Something like this. . .

> *God, give me discernment to know when to speak*
> *up, humility to ensure my heart is right before*
> *I do, and confidence to walk boldly*
> *with You in the process. Amen.*

....

....

....

....

....

....

....

....

....

....

....

....

....

....

....

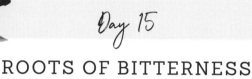

ROOTS OF BITTERNESS

*Be angry, and do not sin; ponder in your own
hearts on your beds, and be silent. Selah*
PSALM 4:4 ESV

I am typically pretty calm, and I can usually handle big stress pretty well. But the little things add up and bring me to the point of anger. I can deal with my child getting in trouble at school, deal with a friend saying bad things about me, deal with a dishonest customer service person, and be fine. But if I get in traffic and someone cuts me off, the anger just boils over. It's not that the traffic situation was worse than the others, it just happened at the perfect time, after all the rest had built to overflowing. And then, once it's unleashed, it's hard for me to get that anger in check because everything else rises to the surface.

Pushing our emotions aside allows them to slow boil into bitterness. It is far better to prayerfully deal with our feelings as they happen so they can't take root and cause an overflow. Psalm 4:4 shows that it's okay to be angry as long as we don't sin. Sin might manifest itself in the form of hate, revenge, cursing, or other behaviors that run contrary to God's heart. Instead, this calming verse says, "Go ahead and feel it, calm your spirit, and hold your tongue." That doesn't mean never confronting a person who wronged you, of course—there are other scriptures that tell you when and how to do that. This one is just dealing with your initial response to anger.

When I do this, I find that I draw closer to God because my heart is one of surrender. I'm owning my emotions, turning the situation over to Him, and letting go. It's so much more freeing than harboring resentment to deal with later. Let Him transform your heart and change your approach to your anger.

WHAT'S UP?

- When have you had an unrighteous approach to anger and how did that turn out?

....

....

....

....

....

- What is your natural approach to anger and resentment?

....

....

....

....

....

- How can you change your habits and process anger in a more godly way?

....

....

....

....

PRAYER PROMPTS

Morning: Pray that God opens your heart to feel your emotions today.

Something like this. . .

> *Dear God, please help me to see my emotional needs and deal with them in each moment rather than let them build. Show me when I need to let go, and help me not let bitterness take root in my heart today. Amen.*

....

....

....

....

....

....

....

....

....

....

....

....

....

....

Afternoon: Ask Him to reveal bitterness and unforgiveness in your heart.

Something like this. . .

> *Dear God, there are some things from my recent and distant past that I know I'm holding on to. Please show me what they are, and help me begin the process of dealing with them. Amen.*

....

....

....

....

....

....

....

....

....

....

....

....

....

....

....

....

Evening: Ask Him to give you the strength to truly forgive those who have wronged you.

Something like this. . .

> *Father, pain is real and people have hurt me. Would You show me the right way and the right time to confront when I need to, and give me peace to let go when I need to? Heal my heart of unforgiveness. Amen.*

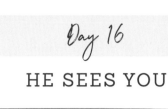

HE SEES YOU

She gave this name to the Lord who spoke to her:
"You are the God who sees me," for she said,
"I have now seen the One who sees me."
GENESIS 16:13 NIV

There was a period in my life when it seemed like everything was going wrong. Things kept breaking down in my house, my job was at risk, my marriage was failing, my kids were going through some hard times. . . one thing after another, and I just felt so alone. I felt insignificant and afraid. For the first time in all my life, I felt far from God.

I was at church one Sunday during this dark period and a wonderful woman of God approached me. Without saying a word at first, she put her hands on my face and looked into my eyes. Then she said, "The Lord wants you to know that He sees you and He approves of you." Then she dropped her hands and walked away. I stood there, rooted to my spot, tears streaming down my face as I realized two things: One, God was right there with me, holding my hand, aware of everything I was going through. Two, it was important enough to Him that He found someone to tell me. Those feelings of insignificance were washed away as I remembered that I am a beloved child of God.

This is true for you too. He's putting His hands on your face, looking into your eyes, telling you that He sees you in the midst of whatever you are going through. He wants you to know that He sees the extra hours you put in at work or at home. He sees the sacrifices you make so you can give and do for others. He hears the longing of your heart for things not yet realized. He is right there, in the midst of all of it with you, with a plan to work it all together for His good in your life. He sees you.

WHAT'S UP?

- Describe some times when you have felt alone or insignificant.

....

....

....

....

- Looking back, describe how you can see now that you were seen and loved by God.

....

....

....

....

....

- Think of your friends and family. Who needs to hear that God sees them?

....

....

....

....

....

PRAYER PROMPTS

Morning: Pray that God will reveal Himself to you today.

Something like this. . .

*Dear God, I am feeling pretty alone. I would love to
feel Your touch, Your presence, in a new way today.
Help me to remember that You will never
leave me nor forsake me. Amen.*

....

....

....

....

....

....

....

....

....

....

....

....

....

Afternoon: Thank Him for walking beside you.

Something like this. . .

> *Dear God, thank You for being the God who sees me and knows my needs. You know everything I worry about and everything I've gone through. Thank You for sticking close to me and never leaving me alone. Amen.*

....

....

....

....

....

....

....

....

....

....

....

....

....

....

Evening: Ask Him to use you to share this message.

Something like this...

> *Father, the thought that You see Your children right where they're at and that You understand their needs is such a powerful message. That thought has healed me of so much. Please help me know of a sister in Christ who needs to hear those words. Amen.*

TYPE A?

*Many are the plans in the mind
of a man, but it is the purpose
of the LORD that will stand.*
PROVERBS 19:21 ESV

Tough choices and stressful times show us what we really believe about God and His role in our lives. Let's face it, many women have a tendency to just take care of business. We get it done. I've often said that I'd rather make a bad decision than no decision because I really dislike open-ended issues. We mean well, truly. We just think it's easier to shoulder the burden than to seek outside help. And we kind of tuck God away for the things we can't handle while we plow through the rest on our own. But when we put our faith in Christ, we need to relinquish control and trust Him to lead us.

Think about a typical day in your life. Cleaning, working, cooking, paying bills, chauffeuring, entertaining. . . How much of your life is driven by your need to succeed, to gain outside approval, to be less of a burden to others, to keep a happy home? All of those reasons, though well-intentioned, set you up to drive your speeding train right into the side of a mountain. You can't possibly keep all of that moving along at a healthy pace, so it will eventually crash and burn and leave a huge mess.

Type A people are so strong and motivated. Those are great traits—God-given traits that bring glory to Him when used properly. God's plan for you might not fit with your daily agenda, but the more you let go of the details of your life, the more you'll see how faithful He is.

WHAT'S UP?

- Consider your schedule and to-do list. How much is there because of your choices versus God's leading?

....

....

....

....

....

- What are some times when you've controlled a situation you should have handed over to God?

....

....

....

....

- Write a prayer of relinquishment, letting God take control of your specific situations.

....

....

....

....

....

PRAYER PROMPTS

Morning: Surrender your to-do list.

Something like this. . .

> *Lord, my day is Yours. I let go of my control over my agenda and surrender it to You to guide me onto the path You have for me today. Help me to hear You clearly as You lead me. Amen.*

Afternoon: Ask Him to forgive you for squeezing Him out as the
pressure hits.

Something like this. . .

> *Dear God, as I pay attention to my behavior, I see that
> I tend to push You aside the busier I get. Please help
> me to draw closer to You rather than further
> away as I face my daily agenda. Amen.*

Evening: Ask Him to reveal where He was at work.

Something like this. . .

> *Father, please help me to learn from the changes I'm making.*
> *Show me the ways You guided me to better things when*
> *I loosened my grip on the reins. Help me to let*
> *go completely tomorrow. Amen.*

....

....

....

....

....

....

....

....

....

....

....

....

....

....

....

....

LET IT SHINE

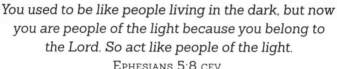

*You used to be like people living in the dark, but now
you are people of the light because you belong to
the Lord. So act like people of the light.*
EPHESIANS 5:8 CEV

Some days it seems futile to even try to live a Christlike life among my neighbors, friends, coworkers, and even my extended family. Between pornography, bad language, immodest dress, violence, assault, substance abuse, abortion, and all the other cultural things that run contrary to the Word of God, it can feel like we women don't stand a chance at being a voice to the hurting world around us.

So, do we throw up our arms in defeat and accept that nothing we do will make a difference? Of course not. The last part of that verse tells us exactly what to do. We are to act like people of the light. We need to live out the truth and shine the light of Jesus. Perhaps for you this means turning away from the media and focusing more on the reality right around you. Maybe it means that you make some changes to your own lifestyle so your witness carries more weight. Or maybe it means that you recharge your batteries with more Bible study and prayer so your light shines brighter than ever.

The world is a scary place sometimes, and sometimes our efforts seem futile, but you definitely miss 100 percent of the chances you don't take. If you do nothing, you will absolutely see zero results. But if you put yourself out there and take a chance to shine for Jesus out of obedience to Him, He can make a difference through you.

WHAT'S UP?

- How bright is your light right now?

....
....
....
....
....

- What issues make you want to hide your light in the corner and not bother trying?

....
....
....
....

- What are some ways you can shine more brightly and make a difference?

....
....
....
....

PRAYER PROMPTS

Morning: Pray that God will brighten your light.

Something like this. . .

> *Dear God, my faith feels dim these days. I know my heart is weak. Please invigorate me with new focus and energy to shine for You. Amen.*

....

....

....

....

....

....

....

....

....

....

....

....

....

....

Afternoon : Ask God to keep your light glowing all day.

Something like this. . .

> *Dear God, as the day progresses, I feel my flame flickering.*
> *It's just disheartening to see people so uninterested in*
> *faith. Give me a glimpse into Your plans so I can*
> *brighten the world around me. Amen.*

....

....

....

....

....

....

....

....

....

....

....

....

....

....

....

DAY 18

Evening: Ask Him to show you how.

Something like this. . .

> *Father, I'm open to what You have for me or want from me.*
> *Please show me the direction You would have me go,*
> *and I will do it with a happy heart. Amen.*

....
....
....
....
....
....
....
....
....
....
....
....
....
....
....
....
....
....

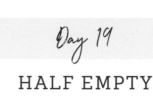

HALF EMPTY

*"I am coming to you now, but I say these things while
I am still in the world, so that they may have
the full measure of my joy within them."*
JOHN 17:13 NIV

"Just fill it halfway," you say to the waitress as she holds the steaming pot of coffee over your empty cup. Have you ever noticed that servers rarely stop at the half-full mark? They go just over that in an effort to appear generous and to make sure you have what you really want. And don't you do the same with your guests? You don't want them to feel rushed to leave or like you're not gracious, so you overfill—you'd rather lavish waste on them than have them leave wanting for more or feeling pushed out too soon.

What if we applied that truth to the struggles in our relationships with others? We would watch for ways to bless instead when our friend or spouse says, "No, it's okay. I'm fine." We'd press in and make sure we were offering a full measure of friendship, not just filling their cup half full.

When it comes to our relationship with God, He wants to pour out huge doses of grace and goodness until our cup overflows. If we let Him. But sometimes we keep our hands over our cup, limiting what we'll receive from Him. Sometimes we stay too busy; we don't give the opportunity for God to work. Sometimes we limit Him by giving up too soon—before the breakthrough. If your hand is blocking His blessing by something you're doing or not doing, it's time to move into that ready position, expectant for what the Lord will do.

WHAT'S UP?

- What are some of the gifts God wants to give you?

....

....

....

....

....

- How are you holding your hand over your cup, limiting God's gifts?

....

....

....

....

....

- How can you better position yourself to fully receive from Him?

....

....

....

....

....

PRAYER PROMPTS

Morning: Pray that God will help you see where you are limiting Him.

Something like this. . .

> *Dear God, I don't know how I'm getting in the way of*
> *Your fullness. Please show me what actions I do*
> *or thoughts I have that get in the way. Amen.*

Afternoon : Ask God to open you to receive.

Something like this. . .

> *Dear God, I want to receive the fullness of Your joy and every other gift You have for me. Please help me to open my heart and my life to receive from You. Amen.*

Evening: Ask Him to forgive you for the times you pushed Him away.

Something like this. . .

> *Dear Jesus, forgive me for the ways I've blocked the best*
> *You had for me. Help me to see the ways that I prevent*
> *my cup from being filled to overflowing with all I*
> *need to have the best of You. I stand ready to*
> *receive all You have for me. Amen.*

COPING WITH PAIN

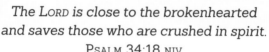

*The LORD is close to the brokenhearted
and saves those who are crushed in spirit.*
PSALM 34:18 NIV

Sister, it's okay to cry. It's okay to be real. Your shoulders are strong, but they were never intended to bear the yoke of pain alone. Your fears and your heartache are near to God's heart, and He created community to help you shoulder the burden.

Don't be afraid to let your close friends know what you're dealing with. It doesn't matter if you're a leader in your church, the pastor's wife, or the pastor yourself. You are human and are promised to face struggles of all kinds in this life. No one thinks you're immune. Further, when you're transparent about what you're going through, it makes other people feel better about their own situations and pain.

But, in the midst of the situation you're facing, hold on to your core values. Don't let the continuing crisis wear you down. Did you believe before that God knew you, right down to the number of hairs on your head? He still does.

Never give up. Keep moving ahead, and don't pull out of the good things in your life. Face them, admit your struggles, and embrace growth. Try new things when old things aren't working. Stick with the things you know are right. Eventually this dark moment will pass, and you'll have grown closer to Jesus because you determined to trust in Him and lean on Him in pain.

WHAT'S UP?

- Begin to write in a journal. Outline what you're feeling.

....

....

....

....

- What pains or issues have you kept hidden out of fear of being authentic?

....

....

....

....

- Write the name of someone you can trust. Now, write the verbiage you might use to share your burden.

....

....

....

....

....

PRAYER PROMPTS

Morning: Pray that God will give you courage to be vulnerable.

Something like this. . .

> *Dear God, vulnerability is difficult in this world when it feels like everyone is judging. Please help me to trust in others so I can be authentic and help them learn through the way I deal with hard times. Amen.*

....

....

....

....

....

....

....

....

....

....

....

....

....

....

Afternoon: Ask Him to strengthen you for your struggle.

Something like this. . .

> *Dear God, some things just weigh so heavily on me.
> Please help me be strong as I face my challenges
> and trust in You to meet my needs. Amen.*

Evening: Ask Him to develop long-term authenticity in you.

Something like this. . .

> *Father, I believe that transparency is ultimately honesty.*
> *Help me to trust You enough that I can be transparent*
> *with others, letting them see my weakness so*
> *they can see Your power. Amen.*

TAKE IT BACK

He who guards his mouth and
his tongue guards himself from troubles.
Proverbs 21:23 amp

Ever say something you immediately wished you could take back?

Yep, me too! To my kids, my spouse, my friends, and my coworkers, among others. As soon as the snippy comment or rude question flies from my lips, I feel regret. Sometimes I have the ability to immediately apologize and correct the situation; sometimes it takes a lot longer. But then I worry: How many good things does it take to override that one bad? Is it even possible to make up for it? Will this be what my son takes into his adulthood? Will my daughter's self-esteem be forever wrecked because of that comment I made? Will my friend ever forgive me? Will that waitress have a bad day now? Those are the questions I ask myself when I mess up.

You too, huh?

Words that fly off our tongues in rash moments can do a lot of damage. We need to keep a tight rein on our mouths. It's so important that God addresses it over and over in scripture. There is power in our spoken words. Power to give life and hope to someone or the power to destroy them. Our words can impart security and confidence, helping to shape an expectation of personal success. Or they can rock the foundation of self-esteem and stir up doubt and low expectations.

And when we mess up, because we will, two little words go a long way—I'm sorry. Apologize as soon as you realize you have spoken hurtfully. Acknowledgment and remorse go a long way toward repairing any damage caused by hurtful words.

WHAT'S UP?

- When have your words caused damage to a relationship?

....
....
....
....
....

- How did you deal with it?

....
....
....
....
....

- How can you keep better control of your tongue in the future?

....
....
....
....
....

PRAYER PROMPTS

Morning: Pray that God will help you control your speech.

Something like this. . .

*Dear God, as I approach this day, please help me control
my tongue and be aware of the feelings of others.
Help me to say only uplifting things. Amen.*

Afternoon: Pray for opportunities to encourage.

Something like this. . .

> *Dear God, instead of tearing others down, please give me opportunities to build them up with my words. Help me to see into their hearts and understand their needs. Amen.*

Evening: Ask Him to help you declare His work with your words.

Something like this. . .

> *Jesus, please help me control my tongue. Let the things
> I say impart confidence and hope in You. Let my words
> be a light that only points people to You. Amen.*

....

....

....

....

....

....

....

....

....

....

....

....

....

....

Day 22

KEEPING UP

And he said to them, "Take care, and be on your guard against all covetousness, for one's life does not consist in the abundance of his possessions."
LUKE 12:15 ESV

One's life does not consist in the abundance of his possessions? Then why does it seem like people are measured by the size of their house or the luxuries in their car or the number of vacations they take or the clothes and jewelry they wear? Whatever we have, it's not enough—there's always a newer version of an electronic device or a reason to upgrade a house or car. And for those who struggle to make ends meet, that drive to obtain material possessions in order to fit in usually leads to mountains of debt.

So how do we combat our own drive to try to keep up with everyone else? Much of this issue comes down to entitlement, insecurity, and the inability to live with unmet desires. The first line of defense against material entrapment is to recognize that no possession or thing is a right. Just because you work hard, it doesn't mean you "deserve" a Mercedes like the neighbors have. Second, recognize that much of the perceived need to keep up with your neighbors is driven by insecurity. "If I don't drive a nice car, they'll think I'm not successful." "If I don't take my kids to Disney World once a year, they'll think we're broke." The simple answer is, so what? But in reality, they don't think that at all. In fact, in all likelihood, they are struggling with debt and daydreaming about what life would have been like if they hadn't made enslaving financial decisions. Third, be okay with want. It's okay to want things. It's not okay to sin to get them (debt, overworking, etc.).

The greatest riches you can have are found in the grace of Jesus Christ. There's nothing on earth that can satisfy like His mercy in your life. Turn to Him for eternal fulfillment that will never fade.

WHAT'S UP?

- Do you feel that you deserve material things? Why?

....

....

....

....

....

- Make a list of the things you own now or have owned in the past that have enslaved you.

....

....

....

....

- How can you apply godly principles to your financial decisions?

....

....

....

....

PRAYER PROMPTS

Morning: Pray that God will show you His riches.

Something like this. . .

> *Dear God, thank You for Your grace and mercy.*
> *Please remind me today that Your eternal blessing*
> *is far greater than any earthly reward. Amen.*

....

....

....

....

....

....

....

....

....

....

....

....

....

....

Afternoon : Ask God to show you where to put your resources.

Something like this. . .

> *Dear God, You know I've been wanting that new [fill in the blank], but I'm okay with it if You say no. Help me to know where to put my resources to bless others. Amen.*

....

....

....

....

....

....

....

....

....

....

....

....

....

....

....

Evening: Ask Him to reveal the things you're holding too tightly.

Something like this. . .

> *Jesus, please help me be a good steward of the blessings
> You've given. Help me to loosen my grip on my things
> so You can use them for Your glory. Amen.*

PRAYERS OF FAITH

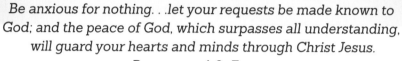

Be anxious for nothing. . .let your requests be made known to God; and the peace of God, which surpasses all understanding, will guard your hearts and minds through Christ Jesus.
PHILIPPIANS 4:6–7 NKJV

According to God's Word, there is nothing you should be anxious for. That means you're not to worry, fear, fret, stress. . . Is that even possible? YES! The remedy for anxiety is prayer and making known every need to the Lord. When you do so, you are not guaranteed a joyride by any means, but you are promised the gift of God's perfect peace in your situation, and God never goes back on a promise. Your surrender to Him in prayer is like a funnel for His peace and provision.

You can see God's faithful provision in every situation you face if you look for it. Every time you thought you'd hit rock bottom and cried out to Him, He heard you and lifted you out of the pit. One time, I was struggling so badly as a single mom. I was alone, raising my kids without financial help, and just flat-out struggling. I remember the moment well. I was in my car driving toward my house, and I thought of a five-hundred-dollar payment I was owed from two years prior. I prayed this exactly: *Okay, God, You know my needs and You know where that check is on this planet. Would You just put it in my mailbox? Please?* When I got home, I checked the mail, and there it was.

When anxieties arise in your home, what does the scenario look like? Are emotions flying high, with voices raised? Is prayer for God's peace at all present? Create a new plan for handling stress in your family by making instant verbalized prayer a practice. Post scriptures around your home such as Philippians 4:6–7 or 1 Thessalonians 5:16–18 as a reminder of God's desired approach to handling stress, so that God's peace will rule instead of anxiety.

WHAT'S UP?

- When has God answered your prayer the way you hoped He would?

....
....
....
....

- When has His answer been different than you'd hoped but clearly best?

....
....
....
....

- Write a prayer of expectation, showing God a surrendered heart that believes prayer will be answered.

....
....
....
....

PRAYER PROMPTS

Morning: Pray that you will trust Him more.

Something like this. . .

> *Dear God, please help me to trust You with my needs today. I want to rely on You and believe that You hear me. Will You show me? Amen.*

....

....

....

....

....

....

....

....

....

....

....

....

....

....

....

Afternoon : Pray for someone else.

Something like this. . .

> *Dear God, You know what's going on with*
> *[insert name]. Please help my friend rely on You.*
> *Let this situation be used for Your glory. Amen.*

....

....

....

....

....

....

....

....

....

....

....

....

....

....

....

....

Evening: Pray for specific needs.

Something like this. . .

> *Dear God, it feels strange to ask You for the things I need because You already know. But, in obedience, I'm coming to You with my specific needs. [List them.] Amen.*

....

....

....

....

....

....

....

....

....

....

....

....

....

....

....

....

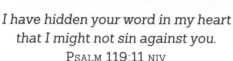

Day 24

HIDE GOD'S WORD

*I have hidden your word in my heart
that I might not sin against you.*
PSALM 119:11 NIV

When we study the Word of God, we learn more about Him and what He wants for us. We learn about His story and His promises. And we grow our faith as we see what He has done. As we meditate on it, we receive His wisdom specific for us as He speaks into our circumstances. Then there's an even deeper level of intimacy that calls us to memorize His words.

I have studied scripture for years and years. I've pored over manuscripts and concordances. I've read into the original languages just to make sure I didn't miss anything. And, in the process, a lot of that scripture has become hidden in my heart. Some of it because I've heard it preached and read it myself with enough repetition that it became memorized. Other verses spoke to me so much that I purposed to memorize them.

A friend's daughter was abducted on her way home from middle school many years ago. She was physically attacked and raped. The entire time the assault was happening, she was reciting scripture that she had memorized since preschool. She said that it lifted her out of the moment and placed her in the hands of Jesus. It was hidden in her heart and there for her comfort and peace in her time of greatest need.

Hide the Word in your heart so you will know Him well and be able to call upon His promises in your times of need.

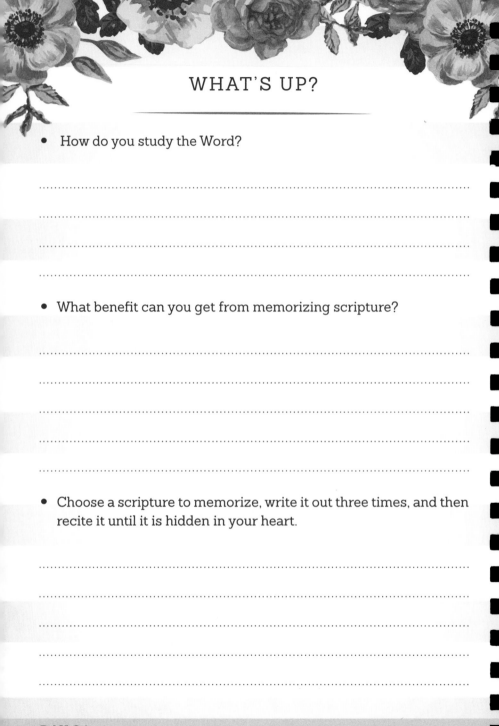

WHAT'S UP?

- How do you study the Word?

....

....

....

....

- What benefit can you get from memorizing scripture?

....

....

....

....

- Choose a scripture to memorize, write it out three times, and then recite it until it is hidden in your heart.

....

....

....

....

PRAYER PROMPTS

Morning: Pray scripture prayer #1.

Something like this. . .

> *"Our Father in heaven, hallowed be your name,*
> *your kingdom come, your will be done, on earth as it is*
> *in heaven. Give us today our daily bread. And forgive us*
> *our debts, as we also have forgiven our debtors. And lead*
> *us not into temptation, but deliver us from the evil one"*

(Matthew 6:9–13 NIV).

....

....

....

....

....

....

....

....

....

....

....

....

Afternoon : Pray scripture prayer #2.

Something like this. . .

> LORD, how many are my foes! How many rise up against
> me! Many are saying of me, "God will not deliver
> him." But you, LORD, are a shield around me,
> my glory, the One who lifts my head high
>
> (Psalm 3:1–3 NIV).

....

....

....

....

....

....

....

....

....

....

....

....

....

....

....

Evening: Pray scripture prayer #3.

Something like this. . .

> *"Oh, that you would bless me and enlarge my territory!*
> *Let your hand be with me, and keep me from*
> *harm so that I will be free from pain"*

(1 Chronicles 4:10 NIV).

....
....
....
....
....
....
....
....
....
....
....
....
....
....
....
....

IDENTITY CRISIS

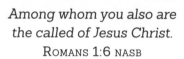

*Among whom you also are
the called of Jesus Christ.*
ROMANS 1:6 NASB

Are you a woman, wife, mother, sister, daughter, friend, companion, employee. . . ? All of the above? Those titles adapt with the seasons of life as your roles change and you become different things to different people and to yourself. Some of those seasons are difficult, and some are so very blessed. Some are both.

There is one identity that never changes. It's your truest role in life and in eternity. And it isn't based on a role you fill or a title you hold. You are *the called* of Jesus Christ. I love that phrasing. He didn't just call you, you *are the called.* Your role as a beloved child of God is eternal and not based on circumstances, timing, or other people.

Begin to see yourself as He sees you. It will make your purpose so much clearer, and your roles will take on a new meaning. There need not be grief as a stage of life moves into the next, nor should there be longing for the next stage or times of the past. You are a child of God. Your true identity will never change.

WHAT'S UP?

- Which roles give you the most pleasure at any time in your life? Why?

....

....

....

....

- Which roles are the most challenging to you now or in the past? Why?

....

....

....

....

....

- What does it mean to you that you are the called of God?

....

....

....

....

PRAYER PROMPTS

Morning: Pray that God will show you your true identity today.

Something like this. . .

> *Dear God, please help me recognize who I am in You.*
> *Help me see myself the way You do and move*
> *boldly through my day because of that. Amen.*

....

....

....

....

....

....

....

....

....

....

....

....

....

....

Afternoon: Ask God to help you put your various roles in proper
perspective.

Something like this. . .

*Dear God, the day gets so busy, and the things I do become
more important than who I am. Help me focus on
what's most important, and let the rest fall
in line behind who I really am. Amen.*

....

....

....

....

....

....

....

....

....

....

....

....

....

....

....

....

Evening: Thank Him for calling you.

Something like this. . .

> *Father, thank You for making me one of the called.*
> *Help me to use that identity for Your glory and*
> *for the advancement of Your kingdom. Amen.*

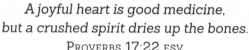

THE LAST LAUGH

A joyful heart is good medicine,
but a crushed spirit dries up the bones.
PROVERBS 17:22 ESV

Looking back at last week, I'm not very proud of the amount of time I carved out for relaxing and laughing with my friends and family. There was some, sure. But not enough. There was definitely some upheaval and personal trauma that affected my ability to let loose and enjoy the moment. Plus, everything was rushed, and there was a lot of heavy sighing on my part. I didn't take very many moments to be at peace with my loved ones.

My daughters love to run to the store with me because they know those moments will be uninterrupted, and we will soon be laughing about something silly as we grab last-minute dinner items or whatever else we're hunting. We laugh a lot when we spend time together away from all the pressure. Even in those little moments like running to the store. Laughter is like music to the household. It knits us together in relationship like nothing else can, and inside jokes are like glue.

I always regret these crowded weeks when I look back on them. I don't remember with any great fondness even one moment of unnecessary busyness we endured. It's in the joy and laughter where the true memories are made. We must plan ahead to fill our homes with rest, peace, and joy. Waging war on our schedules must be intentional, and we can't do it alone.

WHAT'S UP?

- When have the circumstances of life gotten you down so much that you stopped laughing?

....
....
....
....
....

- What current stresses make it difficult for you to be lighthearted?

....
....
....
....
....

- How can you turn your sighing into laughing in this coming week and beyond?

....
....
....
....

PRAYER PROMPTS

Morning: Pray that God will help you prioritize today.
Something like this. . .

> *Jesus, I give my schedule to You. I let go of my self-imposed expectations for the day so I can live in the moment with peace and joy. Amen.*

Afternoon : Ask Him to help you enjoy your loved ones.

Something like this. . .

> *Dear God, thank You for the friends and family You have blessed me with. Help me to enjoy them through humor and to treasure our moments of laughter. Amen.*

....

....

....

....

....

....

....

....

....

....

....

....

....

....

Evening: Ask Him to prepare your heart for tomorrow.

Something like this. . .

> *Father, there were some bright spots today, but there were definitely moments when I let stress make me cranky or sad. Please let tomorrow be a new day when I wake up refreshed, ready to laugh. Amen.*

....

....

....

....

....

....

....

....

....

....

....

....

....

....

....

....

....

SUBTLE EROSION

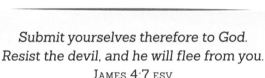

*Submit yourselves therefore to God.
Resist the devil, and he will flee from you.*
JAMES 4:7 ESV

Looking back over the years, I see times when I've walked so closely with God that I could hardly see anything else around me. Then there were other times when I let life—schedules, sins, emotions—crowd Him out so completely that I could barely see Him at all. That change is subtle and can become as familiar as the tide. You won't recognize it until you see that your shoreline has moved.

It's like the frog analogy: If you drop a frog into a pot of boiling water, it will jump out. But if you put a frog in warm water and then slowly bring it to a boil, he will stay right where he is, adapting to the subtle change in temperature until it's too late. The erosion of your principles and commitments are the same. It happens before you realize it, and then it's too late.

There is hope! The first thing you need to do is to identify where things went wrong. Enlist the help of a friend who will hold you accountable as you get back on track. Study the Word to stay close to truth and have a daily reminder of God's standards. And be consistent and unwavering as you restore the shoreline of your heart.

WHAT'S UP?

- How have your lines in the sand shifted by the changing tide? Why did those changes occur?

....

....

....

....

....

- Did you realize it was happening? What made it seem okay as the erosion happened?

....

....

....

....

- What are some steps you can take to ensure that erosion doesn't begin to happen again?

....

....

....

....

PRAYER PROMPTS

Morning: Pray that God will forgive you.

Something like this. . .

> *Dear God, I'm so different now than I was when I first knew You and other times when I walked closely with You. Please forgive me for the ways I've strayed from my convictions and from our relationship. Amen.*

....
....
....
....
....
....
....
....
....
....
....
....

Afternoon : Ask God to help you restore your shoreline.

Something like this. . .

> *Dear God, restore my commitment to You and Your will,
> and give me the strength I need to make the necessary
> changes in my life. Please help me to get
> back to where I once was. Amen.*

Evening: Ask for guidance and next steps.

Something like this. . .

*Father, please continue to show me exactly what I need
to do to make things right and to grow with You.
I want to walk right beside You. Amen.*

....
....
....
....
....
....
....
....
....
....
....
....
....
....
....
....
....

BACK TO BASICS

But in your hearts honor Christ the Lord as holy, always being prepared to make a defense to anyone who asks you for a reason for the hope that is in you; yet do it with gentleness and respect.
1 PETER 3:15 ESV

Satan knows scripture backward and forward. In fact, he knows it so well that he can manipulate it until truth becomes a lie that still looks a whole lot like truth. He even tried to twist scripture when he tempted Jesus in the wilderness. And he is a master at confusing believers. The only way for us to combat his manipulations is to know God's Word so well that we can recognize a lie immediately.

A follower of Christ should be able to quote some Bible verses in defense of her faith, maybe even pull in some outside resources to support her beliefs, and should definitely be able to talk openly and freely about salvation and why Jesus died on the cross. The verse above says we need to be ready to defend our hope in Christ when we are asked.

If you can't or if the thought of that makes you nervous, now is a great time to implement a study plan to ingrain those truths in your heart and your mind so you can answer the questions people will have. In fact, there are really great programs at most churches that take you back to the basics of faith and give you good foundational grounding in facts and truth. If you haven't taken one of those or if it's been awhile and you aren't feeling confident, sign up for one and dig in. Even better, bring your inquisitive friends with you so God can heap more solid truth on the foundation that's already there.

WHAT'S UP?

- How strong is your understanding of the basics of your salvation and the Gospel?

....

....

....

....

- If a friend asked about why you believe in God, what would you answer?

....

....

....

- Write a brief personal testimony so you have it ready to share with others.

....

....

....

....

PRAYER PROMPTS

Morning: Pray that God will teach you His truth.

Something like this. . .

> *Dear God, thank You for the gift of Your Word.
> Please help me to learn and understand it better
> as I study it more. I want to know You more. Amen.*

....

....

....

....

....

....

....

....

....

....

....

....

....

....

Afternoon: Ask God to help you share your faith.

Something like this. . .

> *Dear God, I want to help others know You. Please give me the knowledge and the confidence I need to share my faith with people who ask and even people who don't. Give me new opportunities each day. Amen.*

....

....

....

....

....

....

....

....

....

....

....

....

....

....

....

....

Evening: Ask Him to speak through you.

Something like this. . .

> *Dear God, I study and I want to share, now please help me say the right things. Give me peace about the words that come out of my mouth so I know they're of You and tell Your story well. Amen.*

....

....

....

....

....

....

....

....

....

....

....

....

....

....

....

PEOPLE FIRST

Do nothing out of selfish ambition or vain conceit.
Rather, in humility value others above yourselves.
PHILIPPIANS 2:3 NIV

My grandpa taught me by example what Jesus was like. Because of my papaw, I could believe in a selfless Savior. . .in a Father who loved me unconditionally. In my eyes, my grandpa was an extension of Christ's love in my life and proof that I was enough. He had so many Christlike qualities like kindness, generosity, peacefulness, discipline, and love. But what stuck out to me the most was that he was sacrificial. He put other people first. His kids, grandkids, great-grandkids, friends, and even strangers. His answer when thanked was, "Anything for my kids," or "Anything for my friends."

I definitely haven't mastered that level of selflessness yet, and I doubt I ever will fully grasp what it means to be truly selfless. So many times I've had to refocus after allowing material gain, ambition, goals, and all kinds of other things take priority as my relationships with other people took a distant second place. But, even if I don't master it like my grandpa, I know I can do better today than I did yesterday as I let the Holy Spirit shape me. You can too.

Ultimately, stuff fades away, but love is eternal. The things you have or don't have in this life will be nothing when you stand before Jesus one day. Your loved ones will appreciate that you prioritized spending time with them over working overtime to buy the latest gadget. Teach them the value of relationships and sacrifice. Be present.

WHAT'S UP?

- Who has sacrificed to put you first in the past? How did that feel?

....

....

....

....

....

- When has selfishness kept you from putting others first?

....

....

....

....

....

- What are some ways you can serve others to show the love of Jesus?

....

....

....

....

....

PRAYER PROMPTS

Morning: Pray that God will help you put others first today.

Something like this. . .

Dear God, please help me to approach the day selflessly, putting the needs of others before my own. Let me serve those around me with a generous spirit and a loving heart. Amen.

....
....
....
....
....
....
....
....
....
....
....
....
....
....
....

Afternoon: Ask God to forgive you for times you were selfish.

Something like this. . .

> *Father, I've put myself first a lot in my life. Please forgive me for putting myself and my own needs ahead of those around me. Please show me where my selfishness has done damage and where I need to make amends. Amen.*

....

....

....

....

....

....

....

....

....

....

....

....

....

....

Evening: Ask Him to show you selfless habits you can begin to instill in your life.

Something like this. . .

> *God, please help me practice some habits that direct my focus to others and off myself. Help me to be intentional about serving others in whatever ways I can. Amen.*

....

....

....

....

....

....

....

....

....

....

....

....

....

....

....

....

....

Day 30

TICK-TOCK

*"Remember not the former things, nor consider the things
of old. Behold, I am doing a new thing; now it springs
forth, do you not perceive it? I will make a way
in the wilderness and rivers in the desert."*
Isaiah 43:18–19 esv

We've come to the end of our thirty days together, and I wanted to leave with a message that I've shared with others over the years. It's one that has gotten me through a lot of confusion and has freed me to make mistakes and grow without feeling alone. Once you surrender your life to Him, God is not all or nothing in the way He walks with you. He does not draw the line in the sand and abandon you in the moments when you are weak and then befriend you again when you're perfect. He realizes that you are on a journey and wants you to learn and grow from your failures and successes alike.

The sin and failure and weakness that line the roadway of your past do not define you in His eyes. In fact, He doesn't see them. When He looks at you, He sees you through the blood of Jesus Christ. Clean. Holy. Beautiful in His image.

God owns the outcome of your efforts, and He will use your bright moments and your dark failures as opportunities to teach you and others. So don't fall for the lies that tell you you're running out of time, or you wasted too much time to be effective now, or if only you had. . .No! Today is the day of renewal and forward motion. He has called you beloved and sent His Son to die for you even while you were a sinner. Surrender the past and embrace the future.

WHAT'S UP?

- What regrets do you need to surrender and leave in the past?

....

....

....

....

....

- How can you use your missteps as a way to help others?

....

....

....

....

....

- Write a prayer of thankfulness to God for His grace and mercy.

....

....

....

....

....

PRAYER PROMPTS

Morning: Pray that God will help you leave the past behind.

Something like this. . .

> *Dear God, thank You for Your grace. You show me endless mercy. Please help me to let go of my past and my regrets and my wishful remembrances so that I can move ahead freely. Amen.*

....

....

....

....

....

....

....

....

....

....

....

....

....

Afternoon : Ask God to open doors for you.

Something like this. . .

> Dear God, even though I don't need to regret my past,
> I know there are ways You can use it for Your glory.
> Please open doors for me to share my testimony or
> help others deal with their circumstances. Amen.

....

....

....

....

....

....

....

....

....

....

....

....

....

....

....

Evening: At the end of each day, you can pray in surrender.
Something like this. . .

> Heavenly Father, please forgive me for the times I've dropped the ball. My intentions are good. You know my heart, but I'm weak. Help me get back on course right now. I give You this day and every day forward to work through me. Please show me what You have called me to do. Amen.

Journal Your Way to a Deeper Faith

Today God Wants You to Know. . .
You Are Beautiful Devotional Journal

This beautiful women's devotional journal will delight and encourage you in your daily faith walk, as though you are hearing messages straight from God Himself through His Word.

Paperback / 978-1-64352-072-8 / $14.99

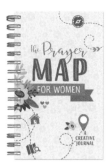

The Prayer Map for Women

This engaging prayer journal is a fun and creative way for you to more fully experience the power of prayer in your life. Each page features a lovely 2-color design that guides you to write out specific thoughts, ideas, and lists. . .which then creates a specific "map" for you to follow as you talk to God.

Spiral Bound / 978-1-68322-557-7 / $7.99